JACQUELINE SUSKIN

The Edge of the Continent

Volume One—The Forest

JACQUELINE SUSKIN

The Edge of the Continent

Volume One—The Forest

A Genuine Rare Bird Book • *Los Angeles, Calif.*

THIS IS A GENUINE RARE BIRD BOOK

Rare Bird Books
453 South Spring Street, Suite 302
Los Angeles, CA 90013
rarebirdbooks.com

Set in Dante
Printed in the United States.

10 9 8 7 6 5 4 3 2 1

Publisher's Cataloging-in-Publication data available upon request.

Why do you love the forest so much?
It's my home.
How do you know it's your home?
It's the only thing my eyes want to see.

*Volume One is dedicated to Erielle Laniewski,
who first called me to the forests of Humboldt.*

This is a book about California. Since 2009, I've called various parts of this long and wonderful state my home. Specifically, Humboldt County, Los Angeles, and Joshua Tree. Forest. City. Desert. I never imagined I'd live in California. I wasn't one of those east coast kids who dreamed of moving west. A magical, magnetic pull brought me here. Now I'm hooked. When I wrote this book, I didn't think, *I need to write a book about California.* I just started a collection of poems that had been piling up over the last eight years and noticed that they all circled around the power of this place. Suddenly, when I wove them together I saw myself in the map: a lover of land, the steward of a state, an ecstatic earth worshiper with a three-volume tribute. It's a personal narrative, a selection of formative memories, but most importantly it's a shared compendium of terrain, an atlas of verse that offers each reader a retreat, and a pathway to access this sacred landscape that provides us with so much. Each poem praises this place that fills me with endless awe and purpose.

Arcata

Held between
forest and ocean,
this rich land
accepts our presence
and demands
our reverence
in return.

People Brought Me Here

I was not called to California
by the beauty of its landscape.
I didn't dream of its sunlit majesty
or dwell on visions of giant sequoias.
I didn't know I'd fall in love
with this terrain—the best of it
unoccupied, untouched, and left
to grow and roll.

People brought me here. They held
their candles along the coast, they stood
as sirens singing a spell, drawing me near.
But as soon as I found myself
in their arms, the land won me over.

Sea stacks, sands of agate, and golden hills
pocked with black oak demanded my attention.
Suddenly this western earth
spun a union from which I'll never recover.

To Let This Land Be My Cape

I stand before the green valley
and hear it say: *you belong,*
this is the place that fits you.

I searched for years to find
the right ravine. I traveled
the country testing canyons,
listening to the ground,
calling on rest and refuge.

Now, a hawk hangs above me
and my body is a stone
among the swaying trees.

I memorize the cakes of light
that make their way
through the canopy.
My knees are stained with mud
from spontaneous prayer
and I watch the rolling fog arrive.

I have everything I need—
it is wet and wonderfully heavy.

Northern California

Where I learned how to shoot guns.
Where I cried behind a giant stump.
Where I learned to be the bear.
Where I first ate fresh nettles.
Where I learned how to split logs.
Where I cut myself with a hatchet.
Where I lost my coyote tooth necklace at the river.
Where I accepted my role as a poet.
Where I first ate chanterelle and lion's mane.
Where I learned how to harmonize.
Where I learned what it is to be *in service*.
Where I first harvested mussels.
Where I found my coyote tooth necklace a year later.
Where I built a stone path in the garden.
Where I first grew garlic.
Where I fell into an animal's den at the river.
Where I slept alone in the wilderness.
Where I first smoked homegrown tobacco.
Where I made a truce with poison oak.
Where I drank raw milk from the neighbor's cow.
Where I first ate yak.
Where I helped kill six turkeys in a single afternoon.
Where I dug a pit for fire and sat in it, so close to the flames.
Where I first heard the grouse make its strange song.
Where I built a goat pen out of pallets.
Where I slept under a tin roof.
Where wasps lived inside my wall.

Mavi

The very first time I slept in my cabin,
I fell into dreams immediately.
Before my eyes closed, I saw nothing
but a thick mass of black.

I awoke in the night to find
someone at the end of my bed.
White outline, floating form,
not human, but star stuff
and certainly there.

I said aloud with ease a word I did not know:
Mavi
then sleep came again.

In the morning I ran down the trail
toward the lodge and came to a halt
at the foot of a bending bay laurel.

Inhaling the pepper sweet smell, I noticed
rot by the roots, white dust
mixing with black soil.

Good guide, who halted me in this land
of green wonder. My protector.

I touched its necklike trunk, its snaking body,
and said it again:
Mavi

I Call The Sun Umalet

I have chased the sun
my entire life. From childhood
in Florida, through the Andes,
into Athens. Always summer,
always bright, my path of light.

Now I feel the need to honor our fat star
with a unique and holy title.

I climb the long hill to find flat land
beside the tiny orchard. A few sapling trees,
some branches bowing with apples' weight—
pink flesh, yellow skin, cores kept for next year's crop.
Trunks torn orange where the bears
like to do their damaging dance—where
I myself decide to dance in praise
of the sun's new name. Naked
and barefoot, flailing for an hour,
going golden and singing
the gibberish language of searching.

Mumbling meditation, howling
and rejoicing in the magic of such illumination,
finally one word starts its significant repetition:
Umaletaaaaa, Umaletaaa,
UMALET.
The name sticks.

Each day I thank Umalet for rising, for setting,
and for returning again. I remain faithful
even in a scorching heat, the drought
that whips us with its harsh hand,
the desert beam that bakes our land.

Still we orbit its glow, its radiance
gives shape to seed, its fire worthy
of our reverence, our divine
and personal designation.

Wendell Berry

You have reached me
in a cabin built of old-growth redwood,
a hermit in this California valley, where
season is shifting and the false
Solomon's seal looks burnt and spent.

From your lines I sing a song of
illuminated leaves—I haven't heard
my voice in days. I look up
unfamiliar words, move through your
mysterious wisdom and am unashamed
of all I do not know about growth spells
and ploughs. I mourn the mistakes
of humankind and imagine
holding your hands.

I sink into the thew of words
as the forest performs its nightly chants.
The gift of language easily travels
from your Kentucky dale
to this western ravine. As if my kin,
you repeat the names I know:
bloodroot and thrush, bellwort and wren.
You express our shared delight
over a glimpse of grouse,
the greatness of alder,
the timing of wind.

Compass

California taught me not to grasp—
to make room for a path with infinite forks
instead of imagining one bound form.

This long state transforms wildly
as waves bring in layers of salt
that garland mile after mile of marsh.
Bulking green mountains huddle in the background
and stockpile snow to feed the many rivers.
Inland cacti cover the dry basin
while the sun warms white sand.

I live in the shadow
of redwoods, respond to the elk who walk the coast,
eat the nettles' new growth until
the junipers call me south.
I follow a feeling, a flag in the distance where
all boundaries are allowed to blend, where each mood
belongs: home is in any direction.

The 101

I make a ritual back and forth
through a tunnel of trees and fog.
Clam Beach is a whiteout vision
just as I crest the hill; I cry out each time
for the rolling emerald shoreline.

Likewise, I never miss the turnoff
for Frank & Bess Smithe Grove—
a narrow strip of honorable elders
held between the road and river,
a private cathedral that says
get out of the truck and lay down.

Staring up into the rich red trunks,
I lose my body and my destination.
What young city was I going to visit?
Where else would I be but here?

Eventually, I walk down to the water,
dig my hands into silt and rub
smooth stones on my brow.
I hope to see the same white horse
under the gnarled oaks,
or swim if the season is right.

The Key to My Heart

You were the second one I offered it to.
I didn't know you'd string it on a neon pink cord
and wear it around your neck. I didn't know
you'd use it as a bookmark while reading
about the holocaust a few months later.
I pulled that key from between the pages
and put it in your cup of water on the nightstand.

You were pulling onions prematurely in the garden,
pretending to understand their cycle of growth.
That evening as I cut each one for cooking,
you came close to wipe my tears. You said,
I'm so glad we aren't in the city anymore.
I stepped away from you, transfixed
by the white milk dripping from the base
of each tiny bulb. Our story was already ending.

White Moths

I like it
when a small
white moth
gets trapped
behind my glasses,
fluttering
for a moment
so close to my eye.
A glimpse of a ghost?
A pale dot in the dark.
Dainty pilgrims
amazed by fire,
I too watch the candle
burn each night,
but don't need to touch
the flame to know it well.

Alongside Highway 299

Multiple chainsaws harvest
timber in the basin. The crack
of big doug fir bodies falling
one after another, trunks
pounding the earth like a drum.
No voice laments these endings.

Yet the insects do sing.
Summer birds variegate notes.
Leaves speak—the ones
that float unfixed
sound like paper unfolding,
the yellows catch light
and bring quick bright
words to the dark forest.

The highway is too close to my cabin—
loud clank of tractor trailers
and groaning engines, brakes
yowling like angry cats
on the mountain incline.
This far into the woods
and I still have to sift through sounds
to find the pure voice of earth.

I walk the trail to the garden,
sticks splitting beneath my boots.
For months I thought the strange
call of the grouse was a generator.
Then early one morning I saw
his shaking feathers, his throat
taught with passion.

When the road falls into the ravine,
when most of us are gone, maybe
an old and hidden language
will resurface. Even now, it offers
hints of itself when I stand
alone in the quiet night.

Walking

I decided it was motion
that could ease my sadness.
The walk down to the mailbox
along our road—
now lined with poison oak,
purple lupine, and scotch broom.

I glanced up at the neighbor's horses
and said *hello* to a black cat
hunched low in the rattlesnake grass.
I got the mail and turned back.

Uphill is always best.
It wasn't until I found
the bird's nest that everything
came into focus. Tucked under
a strand of blackberry, treasure appeared
as treasure does: habitually small,
nearly missed, and made of earth.

I cupped the bed of twigs, down,
and usnea, watched a few pieces
fall away, and suddenly memory
started stitching a line to follow—
I saw the horses in their pasture, recalled
some leaf I used to grab while riding trails
bareback as a child, and smelled
its lemon sweetness in the air.
I thought of the blue snake
I discovered in the garden;
I believe seeing a snake and a horse
in the same day is a significant omen.
I stuck my finger into the nest,

past the soft center
and touched my own palm.

I said *yes* and kept climbing.

When I passed the woodpile
I thought about the aimless
queen termite, lost and dragging
her swollen body over our kindling.
I decided not to put her in a jar
for a better look—
she seemed so determined
to keep roaming.

All became a list of recollection,
a ramble of endless value, each item
linked to a time, a feeling, to my
sense of self. I let them come on fast,
let each one light up and burn out
until I was back in the garden, fussing
with hoses, and watering the new beds.

Cradle Knoll

When a tree falls, its base reveals
a pit pulled from earth, a cradle for creation—
what was once hidden in the darkness emerges,
rhizomes bending their necks toward sun.

My father visits and compares the redwood roots
to a giant shrine. Has he ever paid tribute
to the earth before? Until now, he didn't
understand the ancient cycle: time and rot
nurse new growth in the wellspring
of this toppled colossus—an entire grove
blooming from one fallen figure.

We have no candle or incense to light.
He is wearing tennis shoes
and can't climb the trunk.
Yet for half an hour he stands
staring at the holy scene. I remind him
that there is no failure in the forest:
one crashing death builds a wall
of green and brown to dwarf us.

Drinking Water

I stand in the kitchen at night and revere the water.
I know it's a continuous traveler—down the drain
into the creek, rising into ether, moving toward the river,
the coastline, into the enormous ocean and back again.

I consider its archaic loop
as moonlight abruptly floods the room.

I worship the moon, marvel at illumination
so devoted to a cycle, so steadfast
it decides which way the swells should form
and guides the tides like a mother ushers
her child's legs into a garment.

Now I feel earth's orbit and sense
the magnitude of the universe,
only to turn off the tap and sip
from an unadorned clay cup.

Company

The dog follows me down
to the riverbed, licks his cold feet
and keeps up with my running.
He meets me where I stoop to find
the fossil of a leaf, etched into sandstone,
and the neon orange fungus
curling around the branches of a bush.

I wish someone with language
could respond to my discoveries.
I wish a poet would trail behind me
so that I could turn and point
and they'd splash and yowl and grin.
Look there it's coltsfoot and huckleberry,
over there sorrel and madrone. Under
this log: the bright belly of a salamander,
a small tuft of elk hair, a few stalks
of mugwort, bent and silver.

I head home, dry the dog's wet fur.
He smells like mildew and pine.
I cradle him in my blue wool blanket
and leave him sleeping by the fire.
I head back out into the cold, follow
the river again and surrender
to solitude with an ornery thought:
even if I had a companion
to tell the common names of plants,
I would want only silence
in this blue night.

Mosquitos

There are mosquitos on the bath towels,
sucking damp fabric for morning ritual—

sometimes we all forget our function.

I Will Not Die on This Land

This thought comes to mind as I walk
the forest path at night—a cougar lives here now.
Oak and fir trees block the nearly full moon.
It won't happen yet.

It will happen fourteen years from now,
according to my dream—the answer floated
out of the darkness, on a white piece of paper
with a clear and solid number: *forty-five*

In the morning I lounge on the deck taking in
the view of the meadow below. With a knife
in my hand I head to the creek, poised to cut flowers.

I'd be happy to die in the mouth
of a mountain lion. A quick bite
to my neck and my breath would be gone.
The finesse of its claw to take me down—
precision is the hunter's gift.

On my way back I stop with an armful
of purple lupine and look up at the oldest
fir tree on the road. I kneel to cut
one more stem. Something large
moves in the underbrush and sunlight
bounces off my blade.

I Want to Pinch Your Teeth

Each time I begin to miss you
I imagine your mouth. I see
each fake tooth spaced perfectly—
good gaps. I want to take them
between my index finger and thumb,
pinch the agreeable shapes,
memorize the firm porcelain—
but you will never let me put my hand
anywhere near you again.

So I climb the small mountain
behind the A-frame house—
the mountain's name is Baby Tooth.
I carry with me a jar of soil
you gave me to use
for some kind of ritual.
I dump the contents
into a rotted out oak trunk, hollow
and now full of shining black dirt—
How did you get it to shimmer?
Mica? Glitter? Blood?
I make sure to cry into the hole
and then I head back. I try
not to slip downhill on the slick dry
leaves, but I fall twice anyhow.

At the bottom I feel free.
I eat an apple off the ground that some
animal has chewed on. Skin marked
by tiny teeth and then discarded—
left in the sun for me.

Tent in The Gulch

I stayed alone
in a tent
in the great green gulch
for many nights.
I could not see
the lights of the house.
I could smell
the apples' sweet rot.
Bear, fox, raccoon,
and other wild company
made an orbit
around my warmth.
Awake in the dark,
I anticipated their arrival.
They got so close
I could hear them breathe.

Vultures

The goat trails behind me
grabbing mouthfuls of coltsfoot
and the feathers of a vulture cut
the air above us. The sound
of such largeness in flight
is anything but gentle.

In the clearing, the sun bleeds orange
over everything, filtered by season's wildfire.
I see this bird is not alone.

Ten buzzards circling means death.
I feel no apprehension
as I try to get a glimpse of their meal
and wonder over life's secret workings.
Is there a rule for who receives today's carcass?
Who declares which belly or beak this death belongs to?

Each detail reveals some unsavory crease
that allows the whole of life to fold right.
I nod upward and the goat cocks his head
before running home full speed.

Lucky Lazy Forest

Humans are jealous
of the forest
because it
doesn't have to work,
it just gets to sit there—
and think
      and grow
            and become wiser.

That's why we cut it down.

Fern Canyon

Coastal church, seaside synagogue,
maidenhair cathedral. A creek
with wise walls, an elegant
and dancing barrier—
curtains of salmonberries
and spruce towering overhead.

Here we must wade
and cross on wet logs, test
our balance and halt
for the pacific wren
who drinks and darts.
Note the strong scent
of skunk cabbage
and find the redwood
growing sideways,
a generous leaning bridge.

It becomes familiar, an atlas
of unspoiled bounty—
a wide patch
of blooming sorrel,
a ripe family
of hedgehog mushrooms,
the unforeseen ocean,
white sand crowded with elk.
Humpbacks move
along the horizon and we count
sea stacks, black spires
of rock guarding the coast.

So much variation in this place—
so much untamable life
that has no need for us.

Horse Cloud in The Sespe

We saw the same horse
in the cloud, I assure you.
Just as I can spot the red bark
of Manzanita, the small
mummified Arroyo toad,
and the stone that looks like
a white tooth, I can always find
the outline of a horse
as a thin cirrus cloud
floating in the pink
moment of the evening.

We slept on the sand, not
touching one another,
and the creek sounded
like electricity all night.
Our horse in the cloud
was alone, charging ahead
with both ears pointed back.

In the morning you announce
that you don't understand why
humans ride horses. Until
this declaration, I thought
we shared ties to a similar
earthly wisdom.
There is an equine language
that is a healing salve
when spoken right. From this
I've learned when to keep
quiet, when to back off
and not ask for more.

Passion for Place

To better know the landscape,
I fill my mouth with soil.
My brow against the hill, my breasts
pressed into silt. I submerge
my hands in the river
and call the curve of this mountain
my home. With such attention paid,
maps memorized, ceremonies
complete and fires lit, this mysterious
orb of earth becomes a place
that invites me to stay.

I Am An Alabaster Mountain

I am a white mountain
made of alabaster, giant source
available and always growing.
It takes time to make
a mountain—eons of effort.

I invite the masses toward
my body. A pallid pile for them
to lick like salt, to chip away at,
to fill their purses with.
I am a summit in service;
I make myself a myth.

Carve away, find my root,
eat from my center
and then take pause—
let the earth rebuild me,
let this ivory well recharge.
Then dig in again and keep me useful—
shovel your tombs into my bedrock,
gather up my gypsum and collect
my calcite. I can be smooth and easy,
an immense onyx heart for the taking.

I Live in The Woods

I have a splinter in my palm
from the Beltane bonfire.
I wish I had a horse to ride
into town. Last night I finished
reading Pilgrim at Tinker Creek—
I read the whole book aloud to no one.

The big paper wasps' nest fell on the trail
and I don't need to touch this one
to know how it'd feel in my hands.

Some creature vomited grass
right at the base of my doorstep
and there is a white moth stretched open
flat and wide on a sword fern.
There goes the slick black cat and the small
brown cricket—both cross over
the bear prints on the porch.

I harvested the burdock—dug down
fifty inches into thick dark soil to find
the end of the root and pulled it up whole.

At dusk I trimmed the new buds
of doug fir to mix with fresh
ginger and boiling water for tea.
I spoke to the valley and it didn't
answer in English, but it did answer.
Two trees are rubbing together—I can
hear them singing in high-pitched notes.
They are stuck side by side in growth,
holding one another up, defining this night.

Knuckle Tattoo

First I decided to stop in town
at the old house by the pasture—
I thought maybe you'd be there playing guitar
or curled up on the couch talking
about steel drums and parades. I parked in front
of what used to be my window, the room
where you taught me how to harmonize.

And the neighbor girl approached.
She said some semitruck
smashed you last night and now
all we have are your songs.

Your best friend stood at the kitchen sink,
your girlfriend wailed as I stroked her hair,
poured tea, built an altar.

This is when I tattooed my knuckles—
a nickname forever in ink
near bone to remind us
that even if we can sing in perfect pitch
we all leave this place
not knowing why or when.

Autumn Arrives

Wind moves the bay laurel leaves,
conducting a sound I imagine
porcupine quills make while rising,
or what I suppose
the raising of a dog's ruff
would sound like, if only we
could hear the gesture of fur.

I want to pinpoint the season's shift
if only to celebrate it properly.
Which birds stop trilling first?
Do certain plants sigh relief?

Summer gives its final
hours of warmth—saved for late
afternoon when I have given up
on sun. Suddenly the sky goes blue
with October's brightness.

Good tricks of light, nothing immediate—
all these starts
and stops to prepare me
for a pause,
a time of deep rest.

Full Moon

That night we sat in the treehouse,
making our first meditation
to take in the white light
of the full moon, exchanging a circle
of breath with the sky—
we both admitted to seeing
a luminous halo
wrap around us.
We felt our bodies float.

We drove to the overlook
to get a better view
of the illuminated valley.
You stopped by the fallen oak
just before the turn off—
you were looking at the fox,
I was looking at the cougar.

We didn't speak;
we held hands tightly.
Slowly the cat moved toward
the dark trees, the fox
completely still, its eyes
two vivid blue dots.

Like a Pearl

Miso soup for breakfast
because fall chill
is suddenly here.

A handful of kombu
from the last harvest
and a purple carrot from the garden.

I bite down on a small
black snail
and hold it up to the light,
its perfect spiral shape preserved.

The Trinity River

We find your deepest
spot where the willows
make shade. We are
all alone here, naked
and no one else will come.

We open our eyes
underwater and see a nest
of darkness—boulders
casting shadows, green
and gorgeous. A thin
brown snake swims
on the surface. Slender
trout are suspended
in the current.

A river always carries
a namesake, but is holy
no matter the definition.
This one carries Manzanita bark,
red coils so slight, floating
and following rapids, caught
in the curve of our shallow dam.
This torrent knows our names.
It feels our joyous footfall
as we come bounding to its bank.

My God Comes to Me

As the light swimming up
the thick arc of the oak tree.
I am transfixed by this spell of sun
that keeps my eyes rhythmically rolling
up and down the big gnarled body, observing
lit moss and waxy poison oak vines.
The golden beams are a surreal wave
and I am mesmerized, blissful, deeply calm.

Until a branch falls on the tin roof
like a gong for splitting silence, a bell
of mindfulness without an echo.
I note my heartbeat for the first time in a while
and watch my shirt collar rise and fall
with a quick throbbing pulse.

I consider this a divine interruption
reminding me to breathe deeper. I turn back
to watch the wind make silver dollars out of leaves.
I gaze at a glow that mimics water
even if there isn't a stream nearby,
a rippled reflection as the branches
sway, and again I find my elemental trance.

Sacha

You always wanted to live off the land.
Steadfast, you knew this
strip of forest could be home
minus the mess of the grid:
you tap the spring for water, light
each room with oil lamps and hurricane glass.
It's not a perfect homestead—steep mountainside,
oak-soaked and bay-swamped—but it holds the root
of the radical and that's what matters most.

You have a gentle approach to magic:
feathers left on the trail, a collection of tin
and thread found on the road,
wind chimes made of shells.
You allow reasonable room
for mistakes that show up in tree house
adjustments, chainsaw repairs
and a garden growing slowly
in the thick forest shade.

With a laugh that rises to pitch and roll
across the vista, a shed full of your
grandfather's blacksmithing tools
that you used to make my favorite ladle.
Steward of this twelve acres, maker of culture
among the trees—you are the craftsman
carving wood into finest form, the one who
brings a fancy touch to the rough side, bending
and breaking and rebuilding with grace.

1991 Dodge Ram

Oh, rolling monster, engine
that rides me all over this land, truck
like a token of rural character, won't you
release me from your spell? Or at least
be kind enough to run. May I never again press
my head against your steering wheel and weep.

Two Dead Dogs

I'd seen this omen before—
in Florida, on that dirt road
behind the citrus orchards
where I used to ride my bike.
Two dead dogs in one week.

Years later, when you moved up
from San Francisco, we saw two more
on the shoulder of the highway.
The old bitch was already gone
and the male was still warm
in his owner's arms.
The woman looked me in the eye
as she carried him into to the brush.

Not three months passed
before you moved out
and as you drove away
I found myself searching
the nearby pasture
for an additional sign.

The Smith River

Damless prize
you are our favorite.
We brought our small boat
in order to best become
acquainted with your glory.
We swam at your confluence,
baptized in sapphire chill, a crack
of cold on each of our crowns.
We saw a bat flying in the daytime;
we ate lunch on your granite;
we drank from you freely.
When we think of heaven, we see you.
When we describe the joy
of traversing a river, we call upon
your unspoiled meandering body.

Yellow

Last week, I threw an old
yellow apple out my cabin window,
directly into the throne of a mighty sword fern.
Now I no longer see its color caught
in the afternoon light. In a matter of days,
the sun has fallen below my tree line.
This means shadow lasts longer—
dawn is not a bright shimmer
but a light shade of blue-gray.

Yet, the folks who own the meadow
are still enjoying summer. Their season
just across the valley is different than mine.
Even now they continue to soak
tea bags in the early rays, water
changing to amber in a glass pitcher.

Still, the sunflower
in the garden has turned
toward my house. Its tawny face
is the first thing I see after
I lose sight of the apple—
a last symbol of warmth
before the darkness of fall settles.

It Will Never Be Anything but Hard

I stand before the canyon
and call upon the wild
omnipotent voice.
It answers:
You are a mountain man.
Be banished.
I ask again to clarify
and it replies:
The people need you.
Stay and be in service.

So I do both.

I let my mouth fall open weeping,
I crawl in the leaves and howl,
leave clippings of my hair
on the forest floor
and make offerings
for the moon—new or full,
the cycle spins
no matter where I am.

Stuck in this animal tide,
woodland waif bowing in the wind,
word after mysterious word
keeps spilling out as my own blood,
my own breath to give.

Neighbor

You killed a cougar before I met you
and so carry a curse. Pelts hang holy
around your house, each wearing
a coat of dust until winter
comes and you decide
which will be your blanket.

You sleep beside the woodstove,
curled on the loveseat with two
turkey chicks nuzzling your neck.
The grown brood rules the yard
alongside two dirt paw dogs,
white fur stained with the rains,
and the pig who digs her path by pacing.
I wonder if they know their purpose?

The dogs do.
They follow my truck down the road
each time I pass, teeth close to tires,
playful eyes in the rearview—
protectors guarding junk,
your piles from the old scrap yard
where you were once king.

A hand-built still for moonshine,
ten thin bushes of weed, two
cabins half built and pockets
full of seed. You know where
all the mushrooms grow, carry
a blade for soft stalks, collect
fallen limbs of redwood and pile
dead cars along your driveway.

Master of your own museum, how many
guns reside here, how many lessons of skill
forgotten by most, how many split logs
and burnt tires? The TV stays on, sap decorates
every surface—a single sip from one
of your jars and I never want to leave.

The Men in Me

Most of my muses are men.
            Old men, dead men, Zen men from the 1950s.
When I read their books, I think
                        these are my words.
Then I wonder if they are inside of my body, my blood.
Are they urging their language to come through my pen?
Are they whispering in my ear
asking me to bend toward their character?
            Didn't so many of them die alone, too soon?

Tall Trees

This is where I bring friends and lovers—
where I climbed into the dark hole
of a massive redwood trunk. I turned
my headlamp on to look up
and see hundreds of daddy long legs
quivering in a ball of shining wetness.

The trail leads to a familial wall
of trees as wide as house and Redwood Creek
weaving just behind. I go to the water
first, skip gray stones, eat smoked
salmon, and watch the black bear
on the opposite bank. I leave when
she chooses to cross in the shallows.
If it's summer, I get naked
and swim there. I sleep on hot sand,
dip in again, then go back
into the cool wood. I follow
the prehistoric loop, worn paths
circling each ancient base.

After this is the unexpected realm
of maples. Oh how the light takes the leaves,
nurse logs of bay laurel, knots of maturation
and all of the moss knit like lace.
Here I found the wet cave and went in alone
to discover a root that looked like
an old woman's face. I stayed until nightfall
to hear the fox, to praise and pray, to stare
into the thick tangle of plants until it was
so dark that I couldn't see at all.

Alone

I always think that the sound
of the clock ticking must be something else:
water dripping from my single teacup
that hangs above the porcelain sink,
a stowaway mouse stirring in the pantry,
carpenter ants chewing the roof beams,
the kettle coming close to boil.

I found an owl pellet
by the front door, so that answers
the question of the mouse.
Thin bones spent and tightly packed
in a swaddle like felt. I place it
below the fir tree, where I make my altar,
where I found a spider sitting centered
with a tear of water as his throne.

Pines sway with bent backs in the wind,
my teeth feel smooth in my mouth
and the sweat bee hovers right
before my eyes to let me know
it's hot enough. The thin blue snake
in the garden, the red-faced skink
on the bench, and the dead
black beetle with long
antennae on the windowsill
have become my emblems.

Today, I took the batteries out of the clock.
I wove a bay laurel crown to wear
as I ate the last of the wild strawberries.
At sunset, I dragged an old metal trough
onto the deck and filled it with water.

My body narrowly fit. I was just in time
to watch the bats hunt flies.

Six Salmon

A local fisherman saw six salmon in the river
and called the count *a lot.*
This made me pause and feel
the familiar weight in my chest
that expands when I think about
the end of everything.
Six is cause for celebration?
I panicked a thought: at least three pair,
togetherness, a chance for sex, for love,
sweet spawn and renewal—
but this isn't even how it works.

I imagine them all singing,
an ancient hum in the undertow.
They figure out their future
by rubbing against stones, moving
upstream and memorizing the whims
of current. Do they notice how thin
their line of ancestry has become?

I could study the science, follow
the history, read every book and check
all the fish counts, ask all the anglers, go prodding
everyone with ties to the river and beg for reasons—
but six fish still means the same thing.

I head home and pull out my handkerchief
along with a dime, a few bits of hay,
and some sand. Then I see it—the single
pink agate, small enough to miss. I scoop it up
with my nail and dedicate it to the six fish.
I make a ritual out of placing it
back in my breast pocket. I keep it there,

the same color as their rosy flesh,
a tiny, glowing spell for renewal.

California Calling

When the west calls to us, it bellows
a traveling hymn and we come running—
not just because we wish to soak in limitless sun
or laze like cats along the edge of the country.
We come with fervor for newness.
Every human heart contains a similar burning ember
that grows when presented with abundance,
illuminated in a wash of Pacific salt.

Keeping The Blackberry Vine

If I ever wanted to pull
the stunted blackberry vine
from its place around the garden spigot,
I've changed my mind.
This is the home of the tree frog—
the one I've watched change color
to blend brown with soil, blush amongst
the strawberries, yellow in the straw.

I call him *mine*
since I know where to find him, nestled
at the root of the tangle, enjoying
our slow faucet leak. But today
I notice his rear leg: mangled,
malformed, missing a foot.
Immediately I blame myself.
Had I raked over him with the hose?
Plunged the trowel too close?
Dropped a nail by the shed?

I lean low and study the wound,
the moist skin torn at the ankle, and watch
him hop gingerly toward the clover patch.
I discard my work gloves and leave
the thin bramble to entwine the pipe.
I jab myself with the small thorns
in remembrance of all the ones I've hurt.

River Woman

I am like the snake exposed on a warm rock.
I hide myself deep
between cool boulders and move
over the surface of wet sandstone.

A salmon swims between
my legs, braids of willow wrap around
each ankle—tethered in a constant current
without anywhere to go,
without any need to leave.

This Loop that I Have Memorized

It takes many shades of blue to get to black.
I stand on the cliff at Elk Head, staring
into the dark horizon, and the Pacific churns below.
Further down, sea palms cover the rocks
and bend with each wave. I know they taste
the best, but hardly ever wash ashore.

I run along the brim and watch cormorants
become silhouettes as they dive beneath the swell.
On the climb up, I walk under the worn wooden arch:
giant trunks of redwood carved square
and joined together—all this time
beside the ocean has turned them gray
and brittle. My ceremonial entrance,
I always pass through with a prayer.
But today I wonder who whittled
the crescent moon in the top beam?
Who built this burly portal and why?

Just beyond is the witch's forest
where nothing sprouts as undergrowth
besides the occasional fungi: red russula
and a few purple caps. Spruce and huckleberry
are bare below the canopy. No birds,
no moss, no green in the center
of any twig. I linger in this veiled place,
walking in the shadows
over a carpet of sticks, each step
a satisfying crack.

When I finally find the largest
tree, I recognize my return
to the beginning of the trail—

the way a loop of land becomes a habit.
My eyes adjust to see the familiar entrance,
a bright scar of grass and light.

The Bucking Bronco

Last year I shed the ideal of love
like a snake skin. I've always searched
for a home to put my heart in
and thought I knew what that box would look like.
Would it not come in the form of a single human
holding me close? Would it not sing
so clearly as to not be missed? How many
times does a snake shed its skin in its life?
I linger in the ways of the past, but so many
arrows point toward solitude and I am not
kind enough to the ones who want to share
a room. I can be the dragon here. I can have
my own fire and jewels within the core
of this big mountain. I walk the trails humming
without interruption. Yet the haunt of love
still works its way into my heart—
when I think about building a wooden house,
when I long to show the largest tree to someone,
when I wish to be seen with eyes that know
the depths of my untamed parts.
Some moments I yearn for the cowboy
who will deserve a ride, who will
withstand my zealous bucking, who will
fall madly and easily into my resistance.

Midwives of Newborn Symbology

As we jump the cement ledges of the salmon hatchery
to feed begging mouths briny pellets,
I memorize the way you hesitate.

Our fingers are stained by blackberries, our lips
are mantled with summer, and we keep silent to hear
the pink bellies rolling over one another in the humming current.

We walk down the riverbed that is mostly dry like the deer spine
I found resting in the fernbrake, and I gather stones
for your mother: green granite and forgotten iron.

Damp clay and a smell of must guide us toward a deep
pool, where we undress, swim exposed to ancient redwoods,
stomachs tight with chill, hair laced with sand.

As we crouch over the shoreline, our skin dries
by the tongue of the sun and we carve our awry symbols into silt.

The Good Life

If you could work all day
without interruption
what would you do?

I'd roll hay bales uphill
to the garden gates
and spread the blonde weave
over bare winter beds.

I'd sit at a drafting table
on a screened porch
with a dictionary, black pens
and reams of paper.

I'd rebuild the trails,
cut back the bays
and haul rocks
up from the riverbed.

I'd braid the garlic.
I'd braid the children's
hair. I'd sweep the floors.
Replenish the woodshed.
Burn the bramble pile.
Clip the mint.

I'd read the books
and finish the lyrics
for the songs. I'd write
a list of questions.
I'd make up answers,
symbols and meanings.

I'd dig the holes.
I'd bake the bread
and wipe the counters,
light the lamps.
I'd get the cat inside
close the windows,
oil my hands, steep
the tea, and check
our beds for spiders.

I'd soothe the dog
while the coyotes start
their nightly whining.

Your One Dumb Tooth

I noticed you around town,
missing a front tooth, pants
too short, no socks—an enigma
with wide eyes suggesting insanity,
a youth mixed with wisdom, a mask
of doubt and thick lines in your brow.

You came closer to me, you asked me
question after question about
the solar system, salmon
spawning, child rearing, T-shirt logos
and the names of nautical knots.
Hold me and tell the story
of the baby fawn you found
in the woods at night.
The rock that split your lip
and knocked out your one dumb tooth,
all lost because you drink too much
and never know when to quit.

You dropped the fawn. You fumble,
you pay for sex and friendship, lose
your mind within the ramble
of grand plans, so many guns, maps
and gear to climb every kind of tree.
An intellect wild enough to change
the course of local history
but the flame of your rage
burns out the core of each idea.

Together we are angry in love,
yelling it all out, swimming in rivers
that are far too cold, walking for miles

without a destination, eating blueberries
and growling into each other's mouths.
I cast a net of protection over you
as you sail out on fishing boats,
your stories slipping into the ocean.
Forever my foolish kin.

A Sign of You

We saw your spirit
shake itself in maple leaves—
a single, small, orange tree
moving in the otherwise still forest,
dancing as we honored your name.

You have become music
in every form a note can take.
This harmony plays you back into being—
there you are in the crowd listening,
there you are humming inside a tone.
I even see you as a shadow
on city streets, a stranger
with hair like yours, the trick
of a body's familiar shape.

Come haunt this gulch
with rhythm in the wind—
sudden warm rain
from a clear sky, a magic phantom
melody floating on the fog,
boughs bouncing freely.

I Am Not A Sweet Girl

The neighbors were all wearing
long dresses when they picked me up
to spend the day at the river. While they
were singing harmonies, I hung
my head out the window
and growled like a dog.
I will never play the harp.
I often answer questions
with a biting tone. I've been
known to hold my own
hand when feeling lonesome.
Once I sank my teeth into
my phone and cracked the screen.
At home I unload the bales of straw
and roll them one by one
up the hill into the garden.
I shovel the horse shit and gladly
chop the wood. But I coo
to the cat and cradle my godson
between my knees. I can braid
my long hair and wrap it around
my crown like a queen. Yet spitfire
is easiest for me and when it
comes time to get quiet or loud,
when the men on the opposite shore
start hollering at us while we swim,
I am the one to rise from the water,
protective and snarling.

Neal

California archetype: chainsaw
in the passenger seat, gun in a lock
box, waxed canvas clothes—
you know the names of many mountains.

You dive deep, abalone collector, see
sharks in your dreams, fill your pockets
with agates and soapstone.
You carve a small bird, build a deck
with timber that you grew, plant
a garden and let it go to seed, fill
your shed with wetsuits, park your
two large trucks in the driveway.

Your mind is a crowded map
of forests, rivers and coast.
Throw a tomahawk, skin a bear,
show me where to find
a spotted owl.

Poppy Petals

I was so excited to show her
the miner's leaf lettuce
growing in the garden.
Proud to know
that it is edible, soaked
in dew, each spade-shaped leaf
a shade of chameleon green,
spongy and ready for salad.

But I only dreamt that she was
here, a figment, and so
I showed the plant to no one.

I remember poppy petals
stuck to her white skin—
their orange pressed
below her kneecaps, a few
like old scabs, some
on the backs of her thighs
so new they looked
licked and placed
perhaps by my careful
hand. Not actually
a memory: I never
got that close.

I do know that I had
pebbles in my hair
from swimming
in the river. Sand
on my scalp
from swimming
in the Pacific.

And for two summers
in a row we were both
stained by huckleberries,
just like the bear who sleeps
to forget it all each year.

The Solver Not The Salve

You taught me the difference
between hay and straw—
I should know
one is for the mouth of animals,
a rich green, the other is golden
and keeps their bodies dry.

You are a farmer and a teacher
who drinks only goat's milk for a month
and bears the wisdom of experiment—
one pig kept in the pen with yaks,
one pig let loose to plow the earth.
You fixed the gate with twine, read
the manual and repaired the tractor,
used the right shovel, pieced together the roof.

I stood atop your bales, overlooking your fields,
and my first desire to be a mother passed through
my gut like a quick and misguided fire,
extinguishing as soon as it came,
but like unforgettable lightening.
I am one of your favorite people, but you are
a singular blade of grass, impervious to touch.

Whenever I visualized your love, it was
attached to images of injury—I imagined
showing up in your living room,
blood pouring from a wound, hardly
conscious, a broken limb, death
imminent, and finally you'd hold me
and love me without question.

Once I baked you a Shepherd's Pie
while you rummaged through
your scraps and tools. You left it
out on the counter for the ants to eat.

The Marsh

Ten white egrets balanced,
a dotted line of grackles,
and a godwit in flight
with its long legs dangling.
Beaks prepare notes in the fog
and give this place a voice.

Oysters ripen and produce
pearls while mussels hold fast
in the dramatic tide.
We walk the path
quietly round and round,
birds speak loudest here.

Note on My Pillow

It's the time of year for blood oranges
and thin-skinned brown pears,
so I invite you over for a meal.
I'll cook potatoes and beans, strip off
thick peels, fill up a paper bag
with the brown lengths, delighted
by each starch-wet curl.
When the bag is full, I'll pause to stare
at my vibrant garden, hummingbirds
quarreling among red flowers—
when you arrive, they depart.

I'll let you catch the moth in my room this time;
it will be back again tomorrow.
You can coax the small gray spider
onto the piece of notebook paper.
But I like the yellow jackets above
the porch light, so you'll leave them there.
I'll save the beets for you to slice, though
I do love the stains they make on my skin.

You put a note on my pillow
after we are full. I'll read it
just as you round the corner
at the end of the block. You always
stop there to stare at the giant cottonwood.
I know you are in awe of all beauty.
You are good company, a kind man, careful
and slow. But you should have written more.
You know that a poet loves to read and read.

Forest Home Haiku

I.

Blue snakeskin dried flat
and the papery bee comb
on my windowsill

II.

What the light does catch—
shadow of time and blink of
golden spider web

III.

Dream of spirits here
let light outline their presence
in the laurel trees

IV.

My tiny temple,
cabin in the wild wood,
hold me like a home

Where I Thought of Marriage

We arrive and the grove of alder
is reflected in your eyes
as you park and jump out of the truck
inhaling like a madman. You run up the trail
naming scents caught on the breeze—*the nose is god!*

I stop to see the first Trillium, its white tongue
lapping up the green. I plunge my hand into
mole holes to squeeze soil, like it's my job
to feel earth on my skin. In the largest heap
I discover an earthworm, then put him back
under his dark hill, in awe of anything
so small and sinless.

We march up the side of Wedding Rock
after sitting silently in a small, damp cave.
Your nose is covered in pollen
and my palms are marked with black. Brave
and dumb we dangle our legs over the edge
of the continent, watching the waves
and pointing out the one succulent
daring enough to grow on the brim.
It hangs freely into the salt, saying *yes.*

Devil's Elbow

Rushing river that hooks
around black rock and cuts
its course with a sharp bend.
I was brought here
by three different lovers.
Once to burn branches on the shore.
Once to remove our clothes
and swim all the way across.
Once to jump from the highest rock
so that I would follow.

The fire wouldn't start.
The other side was swamp.
The rock was not that high.
The devil is in the memories,
a shadow of disappointment,
but light lives on in the water.

I went back the following summer
with three women. We were well received
by the calm current and the sun
stretching its rays below the surface.
We napped naked on the shore, soaked
our brown skin and spoke
to the swimming snake.
We sang our spells, opened
apricots for the bees and saw
a white dog on the hillside.
I had never stayed so long
without growing cold.
Could it be that a place
with such a title only
wants a witch?

In Yosemite After Your Father's Death

You turn thirty years old and we
sleep in our own blue tent.
We don't have sex, we don't zip
our sleeping bags together.
Your mother and sister
share a gray tent beside us.

I dream that my hair is long
and wake to see a man
walking by in overalls.
He smiles at me and I know
that he has no one.

When you wake you tell me
you wish I'd met your father
and we set off to gather kindling
for the breakfast fire. Pulling
the bark off a fallen tree with our
bare hands, sap stains us like blood.

The sun is gentle here
and its light inspires me to create odes—
I sing these songs when I'm alone,
on the path to the bathhouse, unable
to share my joy in this time of mourning.

We hike together counting mule deer
and Steller's jays. Snow splits
to reveal bright green moss below
the giant Ponderosa. I see myself
inside the trunk—*It's my tomb*.

Up ahead your mother places
a piece of smooth jade on a boulder
to observe your father's absence.
She asks me not to touch it.
I want to leave with the man
in overalls. Instead, I watch
an eagle land in its nest and imagine
joining its brood, weeping openly.

Bats

You had a dream that I was living
with the bats in your shed. My skin
was stained with chainsaw oil
and tools hung around me like a cape.
You danced in a circle—naked
and youthful—and the dancing shook you awake.

We once made love on a mountaintop.
I bled in the snow, all the way through
to granite. Afterward you told stories
of high school football and felling trees.
When we climbed down I did a private
ritual by the creek. I threw my copper
bracelet into the icy water.

Bats lived in our cabin at the base of the peak,
with a woodrat, a broken lock
and a mule skin blanket. You stoked our fire
while I stared at their small folded wings.

A Poem Before Eating Chicken

In the bed of yarrow
that sprawls the meadow,
all white and not purple,
we burn two types
of wood to make smoke—
one black oak
charred in a forest fire,
one blue oak
cut from the front yard
of your grandparent's house.
They smolder to make coals
that we cook hens over:
two birds who we honor and enjoy.

The Altar on The Hillside

I'd forgotten the flat space
under the fallen fir:
my discarded typewriter
dug into earth, unused
candles, two skeleton keys.
Our hidden ground
where I thought
we'd worship together
but never did. Hymns
half written
in a leather-bound book.

Today, feeling out of touch
with my true self,
I remembered—
I took off my shoes,
picked up a hand towel
to kneel on, the pot
of dead orchids, my old
broken glasses and a jar
of white rocks.

I followed the grown-over
ghost trail, only
a whisper between
the considerable spread
of oak saplings. A steep path
leading me to bow and pray,
to arrange the rocks in a circle,
to breathe in the heavy scent
of bay laurel, to reconnect
with our unfinished songs.

I started singing one note
and the rest came slowly after
weeks of work, piles of flowers,
various arrangements of bones,
the positioning of feathers
and many unsolvable questions.

Song—It'll Be Fine

I'll braid the garlic
while you string the beads
and each and every day
will give us exactly what we need.
And I'll brew the tea each morning that we wake,
so warmth will guide us onward in all that we create.

And it'll be fine, fine, it'll all be fine.
It'll be fine, fine, it'll all be fine.
It'll be fine, fine, it'll all be fine, it'll be fine, fine, fine.

We'll wake up early responding to the fields,
letting blood, milk, and root show us what it is to feel.
And I'll try to translate it all real well,
while you keep us grounded in love's sturdy swell.

And it'll be fine, fine, it'll all be fine.
It'll be fine, fine, it'll all be fine.
It'll be fine, fine, it'll all be fine, it'll be fine, fine, fine.

Even as the weight comes from the core of our minds,
delivers us the darkness we always do find,
we cast our spells in building and in song,
to keep the lessons coming for sensing all along

That it'll be fine, fine, it'll all be fine.
It'll be fine, fine, it'll all be fine.
It'll be fine, fine, it'll all be fine, it'll be fine, fine, fine.

The Story of My Death

It begins on the edge of a gravel road
somewhere in green-gray mountains.
We walk there after I taste the wild strawberries,
red tiny thimbles spreading sweet and small in your yard.

You hold my arm as we move into the forest.
Clouds of dust form with each step we take.
A few sluggish afternoon flies hover and hum.
My right hand holds up my denim skirt and my ankles
appear the same as when I was forty-five, smooth, olive skin.

In the clearing with the flat stone bed
I turn my eyes to yours—
and if you are my lover we both cry some
and smile without showing our teeth,
and if you are my child you cry
and I give you the comfort of my calm expression,
and if you are my friend we laugh and squeeze
one another's shoulders with both hands.
Then you leave. I don't watch you go.

I rest on the rock, face toward the sky
and slip inward. My chest rises and falls
rhythmically, my thoughts slow and sync
with breath. My eyes close. I envision
every moment, the experience of each
human, each creature, each landscape.
My body remains warm as I slightly sleep.

As soon as I reach the very first memory,
beyond the recollection of any dinosaur,
any volcano or glacier,
the wolves come.

Perhaps they bring their pups,
or even a bear, and they set to me
as they always knew they would.
With direct grace and instinctive care
they cradle me back into the earth.

Acknowledgements

First, I'd like to thank my treasured editor and dear friend Matthew Phipps for years and years of service. This book would not be a book without you and your deep understanding of my voice. I look forward to a lifetime of working together.

To my other invaluable editor, talented poet, and crucial friend Meredith Clark, I owe the final feeling of form and content. Thank you for your loving ability to pull out my strength in each verse and cut away all that lacked my specific lens.

Niko Daoussis, thank you for inviting me into your home on R Street. You are one of the most gracious and inspired people I know and I wouldn't have been able to settle into Arcata without your love and companionship.

Sacha Marini, thank you for inviting me to Fancyland, for trusting me to live and work on this land with you, and for my redwood dream cabin. Most of these poems exist because of my experience living off-the-grid with you. I will forever be grateful for all that you've taught me and especially for our ever-growing friendship.

Neal Ewald, with you I learned about the intricacies of the forest and the politics of the people who interact with it, how to shoot guns and use a chainsaw, but most of all I learned about the power of unlikely friendship and what this kind of unconditional love can do for the world at large.

To the patrons, farmers, and folks who run The Arcata Farmers' Market: My life would not be the same without you. Thank you for inviting me in, for allowing me to bring my craft to the public, for supporting my work and showing me how important it is. This market will always feel like an irreplaceable home to me.

Thank you to Northtown Books for your ongoing confidence and encouragement.

Everyone I became close with in Humboldt County made an exceptional impact on me and I'm grateful for each and every one of you: thank you to Adam Prince for forgiveness and huge heart lessons.

Rachel Zingoni, you are my spiritual life partner and I'm so glad we found each other in the garden under the oaks. Joseph Nicolas, you showed me the wilderness in a way that no one ever had before and our adventures directly shaped my love of Northern California. Amber Honeybee Maywald, you brought me to Barney Gulch and so gave me one of my most special places that I carry everywhere. Nicolas Mccarty, you are a wild angel full of fire and I love you. Thomas Dammann, thank you for always believing in me and for the giant map of California that I reference frequently. Abreall Goodwin, you taught me the power of discernment and self-preservation, as well as so much about land, livestock and love.

To everyone who ever lived at/frequented the R Street House or The Garden House, our familial connection will always stay with me. Thank you for showing me all of the special hikes, swimming holes and secret mushroom spots. Especially Lindsey Byers, Sophie Mackell, Kat Fountain, Joey Goforth, Liz Kimbrough, Vanessa Mckenna, Pete Barker, Willoughby Arevalo, David Dunning, Jeffery Mcmann, and Farmer. Thank you Bryan Osper for your shining songs and for your spirit that continues to touch us all.

To all of my friends in other places who visited me frequently, or worked on this book with me, and so became a major part of my forest story: Skylar Hughes, your love and support is stitched throughout this work, your moon eyes added specific magic to the spirit of it all. Jenny O., thank you for visiting me more than anyone else, for driving twelve hours again and again as if it were nothing, just to explore the beauty of it all with me. Nicole Disson, your endless awe and appreciation of the natural world is beautiful and to watch you learn the ways of the forest is pure inspiration. Shelby Duncan, I'm grateful for your endless presence in everything that I do and for all of those hours I spent on the landline in the woodshed exchanging witchy wonder with you. Sarah Sky, it means so much that you understand Fancyland and the perfection of my place better than most. Grantopolis Gardner, you are my TOPS and your visits to Humboldt were so important. Thank you for the way you became a part of our community and moved through the joys and sorrows with us, for the way you celebrated the quality of my home with respect, and for helping me move so many giant blocks of concrete without a complaint. Andrew Poyner, thank you for always being so excited to see me and for your vibrant interest in all of the good green details. Elena Stonaker, we have yet to roll in this dirt together, but you, my kindred spirit, are woven into the heart of these poems for sure. Jena Malone, my deep defender, my amazing advocate, when you first read my manuscript I saw its gift more clearly than before because of your honest and loving enthusiasm. Mandy Kahn, my poet sister, thank you for reading by my side and believing in me with such strength. Wade Ryff, thank you for being a poet with me in this life, for reading and listening to these poems patiently, and for telling me that with my words I will bring people to a place where they need to be. Ryan Field, thank you for planting the first seed of California in my mind.

Thank you Jenni Boelkens and The Standard Hotel in Hollywood for having me as your Artist in Residence during October of 2015. During my stay, I worked on many poems that appear in this three-volume collection and I'm grateful for the time and space provided. I also thank The Standard for inviting me to create my reading series Poetic Purpose. This series allows me to help keep the oral culture of poetry alive in Los Angeles. I shared many of the poems in this book for the first time at these readings.

All photos by Brendon Burton. Brendon, thank you for trusting me as I lead you to the edge. I will always cherish these images and our time spent creating them.

My heartfelt thanks to Rare Bird and Tyson Cornell for believing in this project and getting these poems out into the world. I give all credit to J. C. Gabel for putting this in motion. Thank you, J. C., for making my dreams come true. Finally, George Augusto, my dear, without you I wouldn't have found this particular publishing path or such a soft landing in LA. I will forever appreciate your ability to connect creative people and your undying belief in the power of print.